Easter at the Mission

A Cat's Observation of the Paschal Mystery

Sula, Parish Cat at Old Mission

For information, contact

MSI Press, LLC
1760 Airline Hwy, #203
Hollister, CA 95023

Sula's amanuenses: Betty Lou Leaver, Van Wolverton

Copyeditors: Kristiane Maas, Van Wolverton

Cover design: Carl D. Leaver

Front cover photo of Sula: Anais Mora

Back cover photo of Sula: Stacey Gentry

Sula photographs (as marked): James Caddell, Ed DeGroot, Stacey Gentry, Lisa Lavagnino, Betty Lou Leaver, Kristiane Maas, Steve & Trink Umfleet, Jennie Watt, Jeanne Wolverton

Back cover photographs of and (by) (left to right, top to bottom):
Sr. Loretta Schaff (Betty Lou Leaver), Kristofer Brown (Stacey Gentry), Kristiane Maas (Stacey Gentry), Karen Pettee (Betty Lou Leaver), Ramona Ramos-Ramirez (Patricia Ramos-Ramirez), Marina Gordon (Stacey Gentry)

Illustrated by Uliana Yanovich

Sula's official photographer: Stacey Gentry

Library of Congress Control Number: Pending

ISBN: 978-1-933455-74-7

Table of Contents

ABOUT ME AND THIS BOOK

Photograph by Stacey Gentry

Sula, Parish Cat at Old Mission

Why a book about Easter?

Who doesn't like Easter? It is the best time of year—when life springs anew from the ground, and the air smells fresh like a newborn. And liturgically, we have followed the path of Jesus through death and into resurrected life, and we are filled with hope.

Easter is especially wonderful not only in its hopeful conclusion but all through the Lenten season that precedes it. We follow the somber, reflective 40 days of Lent, like Jesus's 40 days in the desert. Lent is very powerful in its own way as it helps us draw closer to God. During Lent, we spend time pondering the Paschal Mystery, a story of the incredible inhumanity of people and the unimaginable love that overcomes it—of forgiveness beyond our capacity to understand. I suppose that is why it is called a mystery. We know the facts; we know what happened and why, Historical records from non-believers confirm what happened (at least, the human side of it). However, "knowing" the divine nature of it all is so out of reach that it ensures at least in this life Easter will always be the Paschal Mystery. At least, that is what I hear from priests in their homilies and parishioners when they talk to each other. (I love eavesdropping; I learn so much about the people in my life.)

Paschal is not a common English word, but it is common in many other languages. Most Indo-European languages, like Latin, French, English, Spanish, German, and others have a word like *paskha*, which means *Easter*. That word, pronounced a little differently in Hebrew, Aramaic, and some other Semitic languages, means Passover—and, of course, Easter is tied to Passover in that the Lord's Supper was a celebration of Passover.

As for the mystery part of the expression, Paschal Mystery, I also hear people saying (eavesdropping again) that it is not like a whodunnit mystery. This puzzle cannot be solved because in this life we do not, cannot see clearly—and solving a whodunnit requires seeing clearly and thinking logically.

Instead, with the Paschal Mystery, people say that they put aside clarity and logic and enter into something called "the cloud of unknowing." That cloud, I guess, would be deep, trusting faith. Apparently, Bishop Barron (I've seen his documentaries when someone plays them at a Mission activity, such as a prayer group meeting) has said that the English word, *mystery*, as used in the Church, comes from the Latin word, *misterium*. He says that when you bump into a *misterium*, you bump into something concrete that shows the divine. Listening to the homilies and the way people talk during Lent and Easter, it seems that people I know who take Lent seriously do a lot of bumping into things at this time.

So, I guess Easter is a divine time. Actually, I don't have to "guess" because I can feel it all around me—in how people seem a little kinder to each other, how they meet together for soup dinner and to walk the Stations of the Cross together, how the children gather their pennies to help the poor in faroff lands, how everyone seems to pay just a little more attention to the readings, how both adults and children talk about what they are going to give up for this season in order to become better Christians or to help someone in need, and, so it seems, how much fuller the pews are at each Mass.

Photograph by Stacey Gentry

Life at the Mission Gift Shop

Speaking about the people I know, let me introduce some of the ones who take care of me and others whom I take care of. After all, loving each other means we take care of each other, right? And that we belong to each other.

The people I know best, those who take care of me, can be found at the Mission Gift Shop. There, I have quite a big staff. (You *have* heard that dogs have owners but cats have staff, right?) My staff is a group of wonderful people.

- Mary Anzar was the first person I met many years ago when I was called to my mission at the Mission.

- Benito Garcia used to work at the Mission Gift Shop but now works at the parish office as well as helps at the gift shop; we are still attached to each other so I regularly walk over to the parish office to see my beloved Benny.

- Stacey Gentry supervises my staff, takes good care of me, and most important, serves as my official photographer; you will see her beautiful pictures in this book.

- I have known Kaleena Scargill for many years. She used to clean the church, I would follow her around, and she would take pictures of me that ended up in some of my previous books.

- Marie Reed is very kind to me, and she makes sure that anyone who wants my autograph gets one.

- Daniela Desiderio has promised to arrange a quinceanera for me in a couple of years; that is her specialty. It will be such fun.

- I don't want to forget Marco Galvez and Liz Avila who help sell things and help take care of me.

I don't want to forget anyone! They are all so kind to me! At the gift-shop, I get yummy food, lots of petting, a chance to help out, and time to sleep—surrounded by rosaries, statues, and the people I love. Besides the church, the Mission Gift Shop is where I most often meet people. If you would like to come see me, the Mission Gift Shop is easy to find. It is part of the Mission, located at the street-end of the walkway that goes past the field to the church. On the other side of the giftshop, the walkway goes past the museum into the church. You will love walking under the arches that set off the walkway from the field in front of the church and, in the back, the gardens. I hope you will love meeting me.

Photograph by Stacey Gentry

And now, about me—

Every morning, I make the rounds of the museum, grounds, and church, after starting my day at Mass in the Chapel with the priest and parishioners I love—and, appropriately, on a bit of an empty stomach though I do not take communion (being a cat, you know). After Mass, I go to the Mission Gift Shop for breakfast and, depending upon the day, I begin my rounds somewhat later.

I begin my rounds with a discusson with St. Francis. We have more than one statue of St. Francis, but I like the one in the Misson gardens, where St. Francis is surrounded by flowers. He loved nature, you know. Sometimes, while I have finished talking to St. Francis and still in the garden or museum area, one or another docent will point me out to visitors, and I often end up with gentle petting that gives both me and them a happy start to the day.

Actually, if you have read my other books, you know as much about me as it is possible to know. Only Mary Anzar knows more—a little more.

For those who have not read them yet, I can tell you my tale in a nutshell. It is pretty simple because the beginning is rather cloudy. I only know what the people at the Mission Gift Shop remember about me some 13 years ago. Yes, I am quite a big girl now with my own set of life experiences over a baker's dozen of years.

It seems that I was always in San Juan Bautista, a beautiful Mission town in the Mexican tradition. Lots of Spanish is spoken here, so I have had to learn to meow in and respond to two languages. After all, I attend every Mass. Some are in English. Some are in Spanish. Others are in both languages, i.e. bilingual. I like this wonderful mixture of cultures. I get to know two sets of cultures and two ways of looking at life. It makes me a better rounded cat—although, I am, unfortunately, quite "round" already.

People say that they first saw me at the cemetery. Well, there is not much action there, so I came down the little hill into town and began to hang out at City Hall. There was a little more action there, but it was still rather boring and not appealing to me. Somehow, I did not think that was my calling, just like many people of my acquaintance, especially young ones, say that their first jobs are not their calling but only work to put food on the table while they are trying to figure out their calling. I get that. I did not know my calling, either, until I heard the bells pealing at the Mission across from City Hall. I trotted over to see what was going on. Though still a kitten, I knew I had found my mission in life: to minister to those at the Mission with the help of God (my Boss) and St. Francis. I became a "Catolic" immediately. I understand that this is what often happens with people, too. They "search" for their mission in life, but more often than not, their calling finds them while they are busy working, and along the way God and they find each other.

The rest of the story—how I minister, how I survived two bouts of cancer, how I lost my ears, and how I made so many lifelong friends at the Mission—is told in my first four (wow, four already!) books, *Surviving Cancer, Healing People: One Cat's Story, Tale of a Mission Cat, Saints I Know,* and *Christmas at the Mission: A Cat's View of Catholic Customs and Beliefs.* They have some great pictures, too—of me, the people I minister to, and the people who minister to me.

Photograph by Stacey Gentry

As for this book...

The purpose of this book is not to present an exhaustive catalogue of information about all aspects of Easter. I do not think that is even possible. It wold have to be an immense reference volume, and I am just a little cat. I only mean to share the parts of Easter that I experience together with the parishioners at Old Mission San Juan Bautist, including the somber, joyous, penitent, forgiving, giving, and prayerful ones.

Neither is the purpose of this book to "explain" Easter. How can you explain a mystery that has remained a mystery for two millennia? What I have tried to do in this book is to share the experience of the Easter season, for it is not a season of actions that celebrate facts (like Christmas), but rather a season of personal transformation. One can relate facts; one can only share transformation.

Photograph by Betty Lou Leaver

Finally, an expression of gratitude

I think it is important to be grateful for everything—what we perceive as good and what we perceive as bad because we learn and benefit in differing ways from both. Except for some cold nights when I end up outside, my life is mostly good, good that starts at the very break of day.

Every morning before (or during or after) my rounds, I never lack for water. When I am thirsty, I can always drink from the stone vessels in the Mission gardens. Like manna, water (sometimes a pot full, sometimes only a covering of dew) magically appears in the stone pots, my water dishes. I thank the good Lord—always, I do—for the special water He gives me every day.

I also do want to thank everyone who helped me write this book, starting with the cover. Anais Mora took a very nice picture of me on Good Friday after Mass last year. Because I live at the Mission, after everyone else left, I could stay behind and spend more time adoring the cross. Anais caught me at the adoration of the cross and took the picture that is on the front cover.

Other photographers snapped pictures when I was not aware last Easter and over the year. First, there is Stacey Gentry, my official photographer. Betty Lou Leaver took pictures of me doing the Stations of the Cross that I learned from walking them with the catechism students. She also took a bunch of other pictures simply because she was there when she thought I was doing something worth recording.

Other people also contributed pictures: James Caddell, Ed DeGroot, Stacey Gentry, Lisa Lavagnino, Betty Lou Leaver, Kristiane Maas, Steve & Trink Umfleet, Jennie Watt, and Jeanne Wolverton. Goodness, I did not know there were so many cameras trained on me!

Many thanks also to my amanuenses, Betty Lou Leaver and Deacon Van Wolverton. Of course, other eyes were needed to make sure I don't mistype half the book. After all, typing with paws is not easy. Thank you, Kristiane Maas and Van Wolverton for reading my words carefully and fixing the broken ones.

Thank you to Carl Leaver for making my words and pictures into a real book. Without that typesetting skill of his, no one would have a book to hold in his or her hands.

I especially want to thank Uliana Yanovich who drew pictures of me for each section of the book. She is the sister of Zhenya Yanovich, who drew the pictures for my Christmas book. Uliana lives in Russia. She grew up in Siberia and now lives outside Moscow. She has never met me, but she really understood me from the pictures that were sent to her in Russia. I like the way she rendered me for this book.

Very sadly, Zhenya died last summer from a brain hemorrhage. I miss Zhenya so much that I included a memorial page for him at the end of this book. I know he watches over his wife, Alla, and little girl, Julie, from heaven—and I bet he watches over me, too!

Of course, I thank my Mission Gift Shop caretakers, my pal, Benito Garcia, and all the parishioners. All these folks keep me alive and bring me happiness.

Oh, and sometimes they play tricks on me. I forgive them because they mean well, but maybe I need to start sleeping with my eyes open!

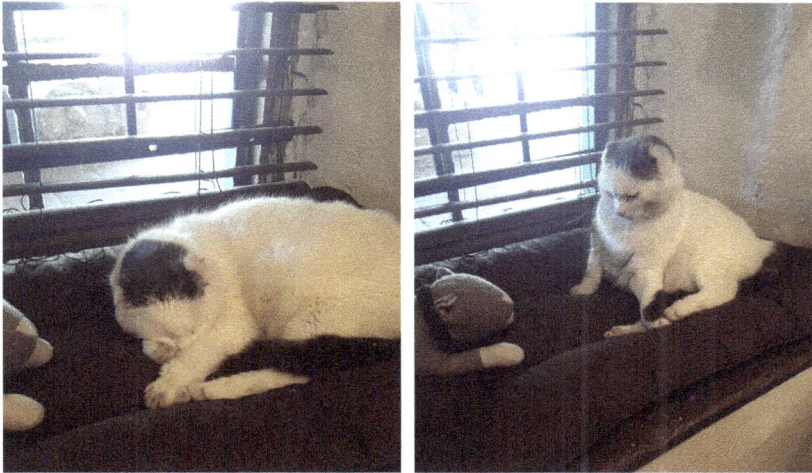

Photographs by Kristiane Maas

Sula, Parish Cat at Old Mission

ASH WEDNESDAY

Illustration by Uliana Yanovich

Sula, Parish Cat at Old Mission

What is Ash Wednesday?

Ash Wednesday is the beginning of the season that Catholics call Lent. It comes right after *Mardi Gras* ("Fat Tuesday"), also called Shrove Tuesday. *Mardi Gras* is a great day. Some cities, like New Orleans and Sao Paulo, Brazil hold huge festivals. People come to then from all over the world and dress up in outrageous and fun costumes. It is the last day of merrymaking before the somber season of Lent arrives.

Most of the parishioners at Old Mission San Juan Bautista just eat a lot of pancakes, but that is fun, too, seeing people do that and talk about that. Since I am not particularly fond of pancakes, I sometimes make out by parishioners and Mission Gift Shop visitors bringing special cat food. Yum!

Like the name says, Ash Wednesday is always a Wednesday. Which Wednesday it will be depends on the moon. Easter is established by the relative positions of the earth, moon, and sun, which determines how much light will hit the surface of the moon, making it a new moon (no light), full moon (completely lit), or something somewhere in between. I may be only a cat, but I know about light—and the Light.

Easter is always the first Sunday after the first full moon after March 21, the vernal equinox (or, in cat words, the first day of spring, approximately). The Council of Nicea (the group of people who gave us the Nicene Creed that parishioners recite at Mass) is the group that decided how Easter would be determined. Dependence upon the appearance of the full moon means the date of Easter changes each year, and—I like this—it is called a "moveable feast."

Ash Wednesday occurs 46 days before Easter because Lent is 40 days long, plus there are six Sundays during the Lenten period. The Sundays do not count as part of the 40 days of Lent. On Sundays, there is no fasting because that is a day of jubilation—Jesus was resurrected on a Sunday.

Ash Wednesday is not a holy day of obligation, but it is a day of abstinence (no meat) and fasting. Many people treat Ash Wednesday like a holy day of obligation, though. Or, maybe their hearts tell them they need to be in church, worshipping with others, as the Church begins the very solemn, very important, very transformative season of Lent. I love to see all the people who come to Mass on Ash Wednesday. I only see this many people on Easter and Christmas. Who would have thought there were so many of us that belong to the Church and are not in the church? So many laps to sit on…so many people to comfort. Ash Wednesday is a great time for me to fulfill my mission.

Photograph by Stacey Gentry

Getting Ready for Mass on Ash Wednesday

The church turns purple on Ash Wednesday. Purple is the color of Lent. There is something very regal about the color, purple. Maybe that is why some countries that have kings adopt the color, purple, for their rulers. In the church, purple shows that Jesus, too, is a king (just a different kind of king). Purple is also the color of mourning for many cultures, and that is the case in the Catholic church.

It takes a lot of time and a lot of people to prepare for Ash Wednesday and Lent. The green of ordinary time has to be changed to purple. Additionally, the Stations of the Cross usually have some purple ribbon or crown of thorns mounted near each. The altar has a purple cloth, and the cross is displayed more prominently, draped in purple. Other than that, there are not a lot of decorations because Lent is a somber season.

I try to help out. I love being with the people who are doing the preparation for Ash Wednesday—making the ashes by burning the past year's Palm Sunday branches, purpling the church, and organizing everything for the benefit of everyone who will come to Ash Wednesday. I try not to get in the way. I think I succeed because people always seem happy to see me in the church during the preparations.

Photograph by Betty Lou Leaver

What happens during Mass on Ash Wednesday?

Ash Wednesday Mass is much like any other Mass though it might be at a different time. At our Mission, there is the morning Mass, which is like a regular day, but there are also Masses in English and Spanish in the evening and, in some years, during the day.

If you miss Mass during Ash Wednesday, you do not have to miss your ashes. Most churches, including our Mission, make them available all day in the church.

When the priest puts the ashes on the forehead of the parishioners, who go up in a line to see him, he says something special. Not every priest says the same thing, but two of the most common things I have heard priests say are (1) "Repent and be true to [or, believe in] the gospel" and (2) "Remember, from dust you came and to dust you shall return." I like the first one better, but I know that not everyone has the same preference.

Most people spend the rest of the day with the ashes visible on their foreheads. They do not have to; it is their choice. Leaving them helps them remember to recollect and think about their mortality (i.e. that everyone has a life that is numbered in years) and about their sinfulness and to repent. I bet the ashes also get them into interesting conversations with people who are not Catholic and maybe think they forgot to wash their face that morning.

As for me, I like to stay in the church after people leave. I find a comfortable pew (remember, I am a cat—I can sleep anywhere, on any surface) and meditate, contemplate, talk to the Boss, or, what every cat does a lot of, sleep while I wait for people to come in to get their ashes for themselves.

LENT

Illustration by Uliana Yanovich

Sula, Parish Cat at Old Mission

What is Lent?

One of the duties during Lent is to go to confession (reconciliation). Lent is one of two times in the Catholic Church when the Sacrament of Reconciliation is required. Can you guess the other? Yep, it is Christmas. I like to sit with people in the church as they take turns going to one of the priests—our Mission often brings in several priests on one evening during Lent to make it easy for people to go to confession. I notice that when they come back—maybe the priest has given them a penance of a prayer or something like that—they sometimes pray beside me. They always seem happy! That is why I think the Sacrament of Reconciliation is a good thing! Sometimes people seem nervous at first, but if anyone is willing to take advice from a cat, I say "go for it; don't pass up any opportunity for reconciliation." The Mission, like every Catholic church makes the opportunity for confession available at any time. Usually a few hours each week are set aside for that. Every week I see the wonderful effect it has on the few people who show up.

Lent lasts 40 days. Forty has a special meaning in the Bible. The meaning is "a long time." Noah was stuck in his ark for 40 days. The Israelites wandered around what is today the eastern part of the desert in Saudi Araba and its extension into Jordan, Wadi Rum (Rum Valley) until Moses climbed Mount Nebo to the west of Wadi Rum in present-day Madaba. Jesus was tempted for 40 days in the wilderness. In other words, they spent a long time, though probably not precisely 40 days or 40 years, involved in these experiences.

Lent, too, can seem like a long time. It has to be a long time because it is a time of personal transformation, and transformation takes time. I understand that even though I am a cat. Sometimes, the Mission Gift Shop staff tell me that I have to transform into a thinner version of myself for my own good. I find that a difficult thing to do—it seems to take very, very, very long.

The Mass during Lent differs from the Mass during Ordinary Time. The Alleluia is not sung before the reading of the Gospel, but rather a praise to Jesus that doesn't use the word *alleluia*: "Praise to you, Lord Jesus Christ, king of endless glory." Further, in some churches, the dismissal song is not sung but rather a drum is beaten with a slow measure.

During the 40 days of Lent, we reflect upon our relationship with God and upon our relationship with each other. We try to be and become the best servants my Boss has. Of course, we never reach total perfection at that; even the saints did not reach full perfection. To help us transform into a better version of ourselves, we fast, we give alms, and we pray.

Photograph by Stacey Gentry

Fasting

Fasting involves refraining from eating a lot of food even if we are very hungry. In the Catholic Church, the rule is to eat only one regular meal a day and two much smaller ones. (People who are over 59 ½ or sick are exempt from this Lenten practice.) I understand how hard this is; I am, after all, a bit of a portly cat so giving up any food at all is never my first choice. I know it is good for me, just as it is good for people, who get a sense of what it is like to be hungry, poor, or homeless.

Abstinence is observed on Fridays during Lent, as well as on Ash Wednesday and Good Friday (of course, Good Friday *is* a Friday). On Fridays, as a reminder that Jesus was crucified on a Friday, Catholics do not eat meat; they abstain from that pleasure. I suppose though, that those who are vegetarians don't mind at all. Instead of meat, many Catholics eat fish. For that reason, many non-Catholics associate Catholics with fish. Someone told me, in fact, that McDonald's added a fish sandwich to its menu just for us Catholics, and more often than not, in restaurants the soup of the day on Fridays during Lent will be chicken noodle or some other meatless soup. In the old days (I was not alive then—I just have heard people say this), Catholics used to abstain on all Fridays all year round, but that has changed.

Many, if not most, parishes hold soup dinners on Fridays. Everybody who comes to fellowship together brings a meatless soup or bread. I like the soup dinners, in part because people are happy to see each other, sitting around tables, eating soup and corn bread. My friend, Marie, always brought corn bread. Then, they would come into the church for Stations of the Cross. Even if I did not make it to the soup dinner which was far away in the kitchen near the parish office, I would always see the diners when they came to the church for Stations of the Cross. (I have to tattle-tale on one of my rooster friends, who also live at our Mission. One time he strutted into the soup dinner. I don't know what he thought he might find tasty. Maybe it was the corn bread. He did not get to find out, though. He got gently ushered back out to feast on Mission-grounds bugs.)

It is okay to feast on Sunday, though. People don't talk about that much, but it is a good thing, right? Sundays should be joyful days because we are coming together into the presence of my Boss and, especially, because Sunday is the day that Jesus was resurrected.

Another kind of fasting (or abstinence) takes place during Lent. People fast (abstain) from something they like. Some people give up chocolate—a popular choice; some people give up gossiping—another popular choice and probably harder than giving up chocolate. Some people do something quite different. They give up an attitude, or they adopt a better one, such as giving up hurrying to their next task and stopping to try to be kind. Still others give up some of their time or money to help others or a good cause. The reason people give up things during Lent is to reflect the sacrifice that Jesus made. Some people make the sacrifice very quietly and do not share, keeping it a personal matter. Other people tell their friends; they find it easier to keep their commitment if others know and can help them remember their commitment at appropriate times.

I have never quite figured out what I, a cat, could give up. Instead of giving up something, then, I give up my personal time and spend even more time during Lent with God's people.

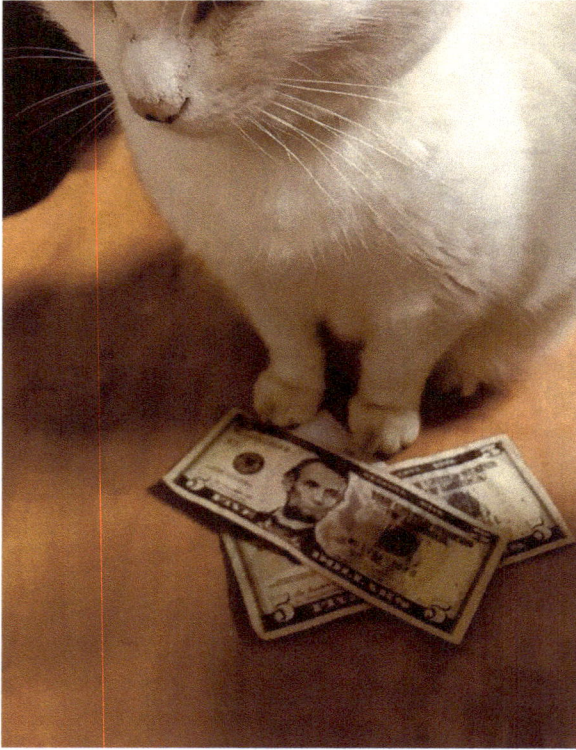

Photograph by Stacey Gentry

ALMS

Giving alms is an important part of Lent. In the Bible, we are told to give alms. It seems to me that is only fair. If we have money and someone else does not, we should share it. That is what giving alms is all about, and it helps many people and many causes in important ways. If we can only give pennies, then that is what we give. It is just as important as a rich person who gives lots of dollars. Remember the story Jesus told about the lady who gave her last two coins? It is hard to be such great people as this poor lady, isn't it?

Catholics are known not only for their fish sandwiches but also for their rice bowls. Rice bowls are those little paper containers that are handed out at church on Ash Wednesday. They are a good way to give alms. Every day you an put a few coins in there, and it adds up. When everyone brings their rice bowls to the church at the end of Lent, it adds up to a lot! We call these paper containers rice bowls because many of them have been sent to foreign countries as money to buy rice (or other food) for poor people who are hungry and without the means to buy their own food or take care of their own needs. Over the years, a great many people have told stories about being helped by the rice bowls.

People can give alms in many ways. Rice bowls is perhaps the most popular way, but people also give money directly to the church or to special foundations and causes. The annual bishop's appeal in our area, at least, takes place during Lent. How people give alms is completely up to the individual. There is no end of ways to give alms!

Photograph by Stacey Gentry

Prayer

Prayer is the third requirement for Lent. If we are to transform, God will be the one to transforms us, and how can that happen if we are not in communication with Him? There are many kinds of prayer—specific prayers of the Catholic Church (generally spoken aloud), contemplative prayer (sometimes called silent or mental prayer), rosary prayers, intentions (a special form of prayers that usually are requests for God's mercy presented in a group), and prayers during the liturgy, among other kinds of prayer. Let's not forget the most important prayer of all: The Lord's Prayer, the one that Jesus gave us. Yet another important one during Lent is the Act of Contrition, which people say when they go to confession.

Some of my friends and I are going to write a prayer book as my next book; we will explain all the different kinds of prayers in the Catholic Church—and there are a *lot* of them. The bottom line, though, is that praying is just talking to God. Sometimes, a format and formulaic prayer helps or even is needed. Other times, just talking like you would to a friend is more appropriate. Still other times, listening is more than enough and perhaps the most important. I listen every morning when I start the day by sitting in front of the statue of St. Francis of Assisi, patron saint of animals (like me) whose followers founded Old Mission San Juan Bautista (and 20 others in California).

I really like the prayer that is ascribed to St. Francis: "Make Me an Instrument of Your Peace." It was written after he died, so he could not have written it. A lot of people do call it "the prayer of St. Francis" because St. Francis tried to make peace between the Muslims and the Christians in the 13th century. I try to do what the prayer asks for: bring peace to everyone I meet. That is why it is my favorite prayer. What prayer or kind of prayer is your favorite?

Photographs by Betty Lou Leaver

Stations of the Cross

One special form of prayer that people perform during Lent is the Stations of the Cross. The Stations of the Cross is also called Via Crucis (the way of the cross) because each station marks something along the path that Jesus traveled with the cross. People stop at each station and talk about the station. There are special prayers and special songs that are sung as people walk between the stations and stop at them.

We have two kinds of stations at the Mission: outside and inside. The individual stations are the same, though, just like they are at every Catholic church. Here is a quick list of them with some comments by your friendly church cat—me. You can see some pictures of me walking the stations. I know how to do that, thanks to the teenagers in catechism class, who ask me to walk the stations with them. I also sometimes walk them by myself. You are very welcome to come walk them with me.

If the stations are done inside the church, I usually do not walk them because I am needed in other ways as you can see from the pictures below. Sometimes, parishioners who cannot walk during the Friday evening Stations need me to read the Stations along with them, and sometimes children who are too young yet to understand the Stations need company. I am pleased to serve wherever and with whomever I can. That is, after all, my mission.

Station 1. Jesus is condemned to die.

Such an easy statement but such a complex act! It seems that Pontius Pilate did not want to do this. His wife did not want him to do it, either, but the people wanted it. Pontius Pilate must have felt a little scared and some clear regret because he washed his hands, though of course he could not literally wash *himself* clean of his sin.

The religious leaders of the day had whipped the people into a frenzy. I wonder if they really wanted Jesus to die, or were just acting out as part of a crowd mentality and had forgotten that their real shepherd was the immortal Jesus, not the mortal religious or civilian leadership of the moment. Perhaps people today should think about that. How much has really changed?

Station 2. Jesus carries his cross.

Jesus had to have been a very strong person to carry such a heavy cross. Even the cross beam, which is what he likely carried, would weigh an awful lot. Think about it. He carried not only a physical weight but a psychological weight—knowing that he had been condemned to die and knowing that the people he had come to save had spoken against him. I suppose people today cause him pain in the same way—by speaking against him.

Station 3. Jesus falls for the first time.

Of course, he fell. He lost a lot of blood from the scourging by that horrible instrument that rips flesh from the body when hit with it. There is something that I, as a cat, do not understand about people. Why do they like to hurt each other? What do they gain from it? Would they not gain more by helping those who are hurt? By picking up those who fall or at least holding out a helping hand??

Station 4. Jesus meets his mother.

It had to be very sad for Mary to see Jesus in this state. How hard it must have been for Mary to accept God's will for this. Maybe everyone, when finding it hard to accept God's will, could think about how painful it must have been for Mary to accept God's will, but she did. We can, too—but we might have to ask God for help to do it. There is no shame in that. Jesus asked God for help, even asked that he not have to go through this experience ("let this cup pass"), but he accepted a very painful fate, setting an example for us who are asked to carry much lighter crosses.

Station 5. Simon of Cyrene is asked to carry the cross.

Obviously, Simon had not joined the crowd for the purpose of helping Jesus to carry his cross. Imagine his surprise—and, likely, dismay! He took it, though. I wonder, how many people, if given the opportunity to help carry someone else's cross, would do it? I think some would. I have seen some very kind people at our Mission and visiting it who have done a lot to make other people's crosses lighter. I think Jesus would like to see all of us following the example of Simon even if we, like Simon, at times feel forced into it.

Station 6. Veronica wipes Jesus's face.

How brave of Veronica! She must have loved Jesus very much to step out from among the crowd and do this kind act. She has set an example for people today to step up when they see someone suffering and do what they can to help, even if it is only to wipe a face. Sometimes, people just watch, like the crowd that followed Jesus. It takes courage to stand out from a crowd, like Veronica.

Station 7. Jesus falls for the second time.

Of course, he fell again. How amazing that he could walk that far at all—from the city to the hill where he was crucified! Did no one feel sorry for him? No one seemed to be helping, other than Simon who was forced to. I cannot help much. I am, after all, only a cat, but when I see someone in trouble, I am drawn to them, to try to help in whatever way I can, like perhaps a leg rub. At least, they don't feel alone. Jesus must have felt terribly alone.

Station 8. Jesus speaks to the women of Jerusalem.

The women were crying for Jesus. I understand that. Who wouldn't feel like crying? Jesus tells them not to cry for him. He does not tell them not to cry, but rather he tells them to cry for themselves and their children. Does that make any kind of sense?

To the extent that a little portly cat with not such a big brain can make sense of this, it would seem that we do not need to be sorry for Jesus, though bad, painful things were happening to him, because he was doing God's will. Instead, people should cry for those who are not doing God's will, for those who have not repented and converted, for those who are not safe from evil because they do not have a good relationship with the Boss, for those who might lose everything when Jerusalem is destroyed (that was in the plans back then—Jesus talked about it, and it did happen when the temple was destroyed in 70 AD after four years of fighting with the Romans). Did you know that Jerusalem was destroyed twice—once before Jesus and once after Jesus? That it was attacked 52 times and besieged 23 times? That it was captured 44 times?

So, Jesus had some pretty scary words for those ladies. I wonder if they truly understood what he was telling them? I wonder if all of us hear some things from God that we do not truly understand? I do. That is why I spend every morning at Mass where I listen to our priest, Fr. Alberto, and in the garden where I listen to St. Francis. Listening helps.

Station 9. Jesus falls for the third time.

Wow, so many times of falling. I think if it were me, that third time I would just have stayed down, rolled over, and played dead.

However, that's a cat talking, and Jesus was a man. Not any man but a very special man. He would not give up because special people never give up. I like to think that he kept going in great part for us. He knew we needed him to save us, and he wanted to save us. That is definitely special.

Station 10. Jesus is stripped of his clothes.

Well, I don't wear clothes. Really, I am a cat. My fur falls out sometimes, but some fur is always on my body. However, people remove their clothes (though I have never seen any do it at church), and what some people have told me is that when others remove clothes from a person, it is usually done to humiliate the person.

Today, people don't do things like people did centuries ago and don't think like people did centuries ago. In Jesus's day, it was normal for soldiers to get spoils from the victim. So, it was natural for them to take Jesus's clothes; they had a legal right to them, and it was the custom of soldiers of that day.

One special garment, Jesus's seamless tunic, did not get divided up, but rather the soldiers cast lots (gambled) to see which soldier would get it. High Priests wore seamless tunics. The lack of seams made the garment not only special, valuable, and highly desirable but also highly appropriate attire for Jesus since it emphasized Jesus's spiritual nature and role: mostly High Priests wore seamless tunics.

Did you notice that the story of Jesus's last day, as told in the Gospels, mentions that Caiaphas, the High Priest, after questioning Jesus, tore his seamless robe? That invalidated his status as a High Priest because High Priests, unlike other people, could not rip their clothes.

Isn't it interesting that the soldiers refuse to rip Jesus's tunic? He did not stop being a High Priest even though he was crucified. In fact, no other High Priest than Jesus would ever be needed again because the High Priest mediated between the Jews and God—and now Jesus had become the mediator (or rather, direct access) to God.

Station 11. Jesus is nailed to the cross.

Ouch! How could he tolerate that kind of pain? Unbelievable cruelty! I am puzzled by how cruel people can be. I do not understand why. Maybe that is because I am only a cat. Maybe people have a good explanation that they understand.

The place this happened is called Golgotha, Aramaic for *place of the skull*. The Latin word for *skull* is *calvaria*. For that reason, people call the place of the crucifixion Calvary. It was located outside Jerusalem at the end of the path that Jesus had walked.

Station 12. Jesus dies on the cross.

Before Jesus died, he called out some famous words, "My God, My God, why have you forsaken me?" How terrible to feel separated from God! When one feels such utter loneliness, it is time for repentance, time for confession, time for reconciliation—and time for Lent, the Triduum, and Easter. It is a strong conduit to bring us closer to God, and I really like all the extra time I get to spend with my Boss at this time.

Then came his last words: "Father, into thy arms I commend my spirit." He was back with God! That is the very best place to be. I like being with the Boss as often as I can.

People often say *The Lord's Prayer* and also sometimes the *Hail Mary* and *Glory Be* at the 12th station. I cannot say any of those, and if I meow, which is the only noise I can make, I would disrupt the solemnity of the moment, so I lie down to show that I understand. (Even if I walk the stations alone outside, I lie down because this is a very powerful and meaningful station.)

One more important thing about this station: When Jesus died there was a big earthquake and everything turned dark. That must have been scary. We get little earthquakes all the time at the Mission. Sometimes, they scare me. I cannot imagine a big one like on Good Friday. Clearly, people were scared because the Roman centurion guarding Jesus said, "Surely, this was the son of God."

When the earth shook, the veil in the temple, the one that separated the High Priest from the people, the one through which the High Priest went to intercede on behalf of the people, ripped in half. Now God's plan was fulfilled. The High Priest's intercession was no longer needed. Now the people had Jesus for intercession. That was a happy thing, I think. I like talking to the Boss directly.

Station 13. Jesus is taken down from the cross.

Before taking Jesus down from the cross, a soldier thrust a lance through Jesus's side and into his heart. Out flowed water and blood. People commonly suppose that Jesus died of suffocation because one cannot get air out of the lungs while hanging. However, I once heard a doctor say that more likely Jesus died of heart failure because the flow of blood and water indicated that the sac around the heart had filled with water and squeezed the heart into not beating. So, Jesus died of a broken heart, maybe literally and figuratively.

Either way, it was a painful death. Mary must have grieved tremendously when they placed him in her lap. Perhaps that painful experience allows her to understand us better when we feel pain.

Station 14. Jesus is laid in the tomb.

Joseph of Arimathea, a rich man, asked Pilate for permission to put Jesus in an unused tomb he owned. (Not all rich men are unable to go through the eye of camel—if God allows, they can do it!) Jesus was wrapped in linens and laid to rest. The tomb was closed by rolling a large boulder against the opening, and Mary Magdalene and another Mary sat down across from it.

Pilate also stationed soldiers outside of the tomb, as he was urged by the religious leaders of Jerusalem. They were afraid that someone would come and steal Jesus's body because Jesus had said that he would arise on the third day. Well, guess what? Those soldiers did not matter. Jesus did exactly as he had said: he arose, and we have Easter.

That is what each station says to me, just a cat on a pew observing people and doing what my Boss tells me to. Often, during the indoor Stations (which are the most typical since they are usually done at 7:00 at night on Fridays), I keep someone company who needs company, as directed by my Boss.

Whether outdoors or indoors, people walk from station to station, stopping at each station. The exception is indoors, where those who cannot walk sit and participate fully from the pew.

After the name of each station is announced, everyone says. "We adore you, O Christ, and we bless you because by your holy cross you have redeemed the world." They kneel when they say this. I sit.

There is also a prayer by the priest, followed by one by the people. During the prayer by the people, the people kneel, and I sit—unless the stations are inside and I am sitting with someone who cannot walk and reading along with that person. In that case, I sit the entire time for the duration of all the stations. Reading is hard work for a cat; I must concentrate. I get rewarded, though, when people, like Cheyenne Hernandez (in the picture on the left) and the Umfleet children (in the picture on the right) stay after the praying at the indoor stations has finished and pet me.

The songs that are sung as people walk from station to station are beautiful. Several different ones are used. My favorite comes from the Spanish-language stations:

> *Perdona a tu pueblo, Señor,*
> *Perdona a tu pueblo, perdone le, Señor.*
> (That means: Forgive your people, Lord;
> forgive your people, forgive them, Lord.)

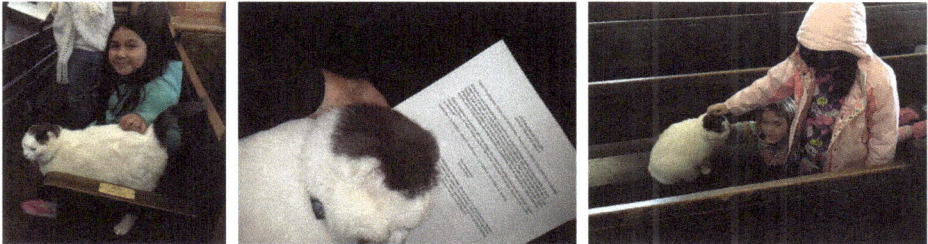

Photos by Betty Lou Leaver (left),
Jeanne Wolverton (center), Steve & Trink Umfleet (right)

Sula, Parish Cat at Old Mission

PALM SUNDAY

Illustration by Uliana Yanovich

Sula, Parish Cat at Old Mission

What is Palm Sunday?

Palm Sunday is the Sixth Sunday of Lent and the Sunday before Easter. It is a moveable feast because the date changes every year, just like the moveable feast of Easter. Palm Sunday starts Holy Week, the last week of Lent.

On Palm Sunday, the priest is allowed to wear a color other than purple—but can wear purple if he wishes to. Palm Sunday is a joyous interlude in the somber season of Lent. I can almost always feel the joy of the parishioners, the priest, and those who serve for the Mass—the cantors, lectors, and altar servers. I get much petting on Palm Sunday.

Palm Sunday celebrates Jesus's triumphant ride on a donkey into Jerusalem. Jesus sent his disciplines into town to bring to him a donkey and a colt, and to tell the owner of the animals that the Lord needed them.

A large crowd followed Jesus into Jerusalem, and they laid palm branches in front of him along the way. Some even laid their cloaks in front of him, making a special path for him to follow. The crowd shouted and sang songs that should be familiar to every Catholic because everyone sings them at every Mass: "Blessed is he who comes in the name of the Lord. Hosanna in the highest!" (I wonder if there were any cats among the crowd...)

The *Old Testament* presaged Jesus's journey into Jerusalem. The prophet Zechariah wrote, "See, your king comes to you, righteous and victorious, lowly and riding on a donkey."

So, what I have heard about the symbols associated with Palm Sunday, I will share. There are several of them. Although we do not always contemplate the significance of these symbols, we should because these visible things tell us much about the invisible world of God.

First, going to Jerusalem reflects the path taken by many prophets before Jesus. *All* of these prophets were martyred after going to Jerusalem. Hm, there seems to be a dark shadow to that joyous day—if you think about it.

Second, the donkey is often considered an animal of peace. I have never met a donkey, but I would think that Jesus would certainly pick an animal of peace because Jesus's message was one of peace. After all, he is referred to as the "Prince of Peace."

Third, riding a donkey in a procession would indicate that Jesus is a king because kings often rode donkeys in processions in those days. Many people mistakenly thought that he was supposed to be the king of Israel in those days. That was not the kind of king he was meant to be at all, but that mistaken idea led to some of the leadership wanting to kill him—and take him out of the running for kingship. They simply did not understand.) Ironically, Jesus's real kingship is not local (Israel)—he reached out to the Gentiles and to everyone everywhere—and his kingship was not limited to Israel of the time when he lived—it is eternal. God did not send Jesus to fight the political battles of Israel; Jesus's fight, instead, was for the purpose of defeating death.

Fourth, what about those palm branches? They represented good and victory.

Fifth, the words that were shouted were symbolic as well. Well, back then, the words had literal meanings, but today, to understand them, we have to consider the original meaning of the words (in their original language, Aramaic). For example, *hosanna* refers to *savior* or *salvation*. That, of course, referred to Jesus and foreshadowed the value and effect of the Resurrection.

Palm Sunday exudes joy, and Jesus's ride into Jerusalem was triumphant indeed. It created quite a commotion. What sometimes people forget, though, is that this is the beginning of Holy Week, and Jesus's ride into Jerusalem was the beginning of his journey to the cross.

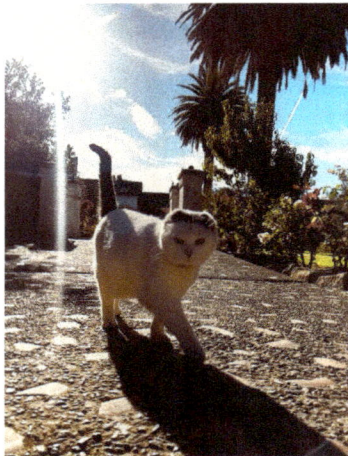

Photograph by Stacey Gentry

The Palms

Here in San Juan Bautista, we live among palms, and I sit among them and play among them every day. I have been told that our climate here is very similar to the climate in Jordan and Israel, where Jesus lived and ministered.

On Palm Sunday, the church is decorated with palm branches. The parishioners each get a palm frond, which some folks fashion into the shape of a cross, that they keep until the following year, when they return them so that the palm branches can be burned to make the ashes for Ash Wednesday.

At the beginning of Mass, the parishioners gather outside the church, each holding his or her palm branch in hand while the priest says a prayer. Sometimes, they form two rows, with the priest at the head. Other times (most times at our Mission), they just gather around the priest, close to each other and to him. I gather with them when I can. If there is no room for me, or if I am needed for someone special inside, I wait on a pew until they come back in.

Photograph by Jennie Watt

The Procession

The procession can be into the church. It can be around the church. It depends upon what the priest wants, I suppose. There are many ways to emulate the ride of Jesus into Jerusalem as his followers walked along beside him.

Sometimes (not often at our Mission), the priest and parishioners walk around the church instead of walking straight into the church. While processing, they often sing:

> The King of Glory comes,
> The nation rejoices,
> Open the gates before him,
> Lift up your voices.
> etc.

One year, Fr. Jim, not only walked around the church; he walked around the entire town (well, after all, our town is tiny). He went right from the church, straight down to Third Street, the main street in San Juan Bautista, all the way to almost the end of Third Street, then back up Monterey Street to Second Street, where the church is located, and back past the Mission gardens and into the church. Deacon Van led the way, swinging the thurible—and spread incense all over downtown San Juan Bautista!

I wished I could have gone with them, but I know where my place is: the Mission. I do not leave the Mission grounds; that is by choice. So, when Fr. Jim led the procession around town, I stayed at the Mission, my home, and waited for everyone to return—I knew they would—under the stone bench in the Mission gardens.

Most years, though, the procession is very short. After receiving their palm branches, the parishioners walk back into the church, which is decorated with palm branches, and down the aisle, where I am eagerly awaiting their return.

However, it is done, it is a beautiful ceremony. Most important, it reminds us of the great joy of Jesus entering Jerusalem that preceded the great sorrow of his passion just a short while later.

HOLY THURSDAY
(Maundy Thursday)

Illustration by Uliana Yanovich

Sula, Parish Cat at Old Mission

What is Holy Thursday?

Holy Thursday (or Holy Thursday) starts the Triduum (Latin for three days) with its evening Mass. The Triduum is a 3-day period at the end of Lent and includes Holy Thursday, Good Friday, and Saturday vigil.

Holy Thursday commemorates the Last Supper. That is when Jesus ate together for the last time with his 12 apostles (and during which Judas slipped out and betrayed him for 30 pieces of silver). Before eating supper with his apostles, Jesus washed their feet. The feet washing is also commemorated during the Holy Thursday Mass.

Maundy, a term common to Protestant churches, is an old word used in England and France that meant "commandment" (Latin: *mandatum*). It was called that because during the Last Supper, Jesus gave the apostles (us, too) a very important commandment: "A new commandant I give to you, that you love one another even as I have loved you" (John 13:34).

Photograph by Ed Degroot

The Mass on Holy Thursday

The Mass on Holy Thursday is different from other Masses. It is long, active, and a bit quiet. People are occupied with participation in the Mass (more than at other Masses), and I sometimes find that I have a little time to myself.

I like to climb up onto the piano and rest near the musician, which is almost always either Ed Degroot or Br. James from St. Francis Retreat Center, up the hill from Old Mission San Juan Bautista. I am always welcomed, which is a very good feeling. I like to think that just like Jesus and his apostles went to an upper room for their supper, I am also "up"—up on the piano, about as high as I can get in the church.

One of the special parts of the Holy Thursday Mass is the washing of feet. This act reflects Jesus washing the disciplines' feet in a show of humility and service. Likewise, the priest washes the feet of 12 parishioners, who sit on chairs at the end of the pews. The priest is assisted by either a deacon or an altar server.

One year, Fr. Greg, our priest at the time, had the 12 "apostles" (selected parishioners) wash the feet of all the other parishioners. I think that was a surprise for some of the parishioners, but I could sense that they liked it.

Jesus washed the apostles' feet because their feet were dirty. Like everyone else in the area around the Mediterranean Sea, the apostles wore sandals, and they walked about the desert. Everyone expected to have dirty feet.

When entering a home as a guest, people's feet were often washed. If they were washed by a servant, it was considered lowly work. If they were washed by the host, it was considered a greeting, an extension of a welcome, and a sign of friendship. If a wife washed the feet of her husband, it was a sign of love.

Foot washing, then, was a complicated ritual—and that did not even include the need to wash feet before religious services. Foot washing before religious services was required because one does not come before God with dirty feet. So, the priest would wash the feet of the worshippers. (Here we cats have an advantage. We just lick our paws clean.)

Although Jesus did not say why he was washing the feet of his apostles, the description in the *New Testament* makes it clear that his action differed from the tradition of the times. He did it first from love; that is clear from the commandant he gave to love one another. It is also clear from his conversation with Peter who, at first, did not want Jesus to wash his feet because he felt that he was not worthy of that. Jesus explained, though, that if he did not wash Peter's feet, Peter would lose out on a stronger relationship with Jesus (and, of course, Peter immediately acqui-esced). Second, washing the apostles' feet demonstrated Jesus's humility and servanthood, and it became an example for people to follow with each other, to be each other's servant. Sorry, unfortunately, as a cat, this is one ritual I can only watch though I do sometimes (rarely) wash a parish-ioner's hand or face with my tongue. That is me doing my best to follow Jesus's command and example.

The Eucharist is, of course, also a part of the Holy Thursday Mass as it is the center of attention at every Mass. The words of the Eucharist par-allel those of Jesus during the Last Supper, and the host and wine (body and blood) let us be with Jesus during the Eucharist. (Don't forget that in Greek *efkharisto*, the origin of the word *eucharist*, means *thank you*.)

All three gatherings of the Triduum—this Mass of the Lord's Supper, the Good Friday service, and the Easter Vigil—are considered to be one continuing service so this Mass doesn't end as usual. There is no reces-sional. The Mass simply stops when

- the container of consecrated bread is taken to the Altar of Re-pose (at the Mission, this is in the Guadalupe Chapel);

- the altar is stripped;

- the priest carries the sacred body to the Guadalupe Chapel;

- the people accompany the priest or leave (their choice);

- those who accompany the priest either leave after reaching the Guadalupe Chapel or stay there; and

- everyone who stays at the Guidalupe Chapel remains in silent meditation until ready to simply leave.

I am also free to accompany the priest. I do. Somberly, like all the parishioners.

These three days, once the Lord's Supper has finished, are sad ones. Even a cat can feel the sadness in the service. Maybe the sadness comes from the Mass being a continuing service and everyone already knowing not only how it will end (that part is joyful) but also the agony and passion that will take place before the joyful resurrection.

Photograph by Stacey Gentry

Adoration of the Blessed Sacrament

In the chapel, the priest exposes the Blessed Sacrament to begin the Adoration. During the Adoration of the Blessed Sacrament, everyone kneels. The priest and the parishioners recite prayers. I will describe the many different kinds of prayers in my next book, *Praying with Sula: A Cat Shares the Prayers of the Catholic Church*. They include The Divine Praises, requests for mercy, personal prayer, and silence, among others. The Boss does not care how you adore the Blessed Sacrament; He just cares that you do so. I think Jesus is very happy to see so many people in front of him in the chapel on Holy Thursday.

After the prayers are over, the priest stays kneeling in adoration for a while and then leaves. Parishioners may leave whenever they have finished their prayers and adoration. Some leave soon; others stay longer; some stay very long; I stay longest.

While the parishioners are engaged in adoration, I move among them, looking for any who might need me. My mission never stops, regardless of what shape the Mass takes. That is why I stay the longest for the Adoration of the Cross.

GOOD FRIDAY

Illustration by Uliana Yanovich

Sula, Parish Cat at Old Mission

What is Good Friday?

Good Friday is the day that Jesus was crucified and died. No one knows for sure how it came to be called "good." There are at least three explanations. Maybe some of you know other explanations. When so many years pass, information changes and gets lost. Then, it can be impossible to find out the real story. We can only make educated guesses. I will share the three explanations that I have heard.

1. The first explanation says that in the old days all religious observations were called "good" (in English).

2. The second explanation says that the word *good* is a corruption of the word *God*, so that Good Friday was really God's Friday.

3. The third explanation says that "good" refers to the salvation that became available to people as a result of Jesus's crucifixion.

Most languages other than English use the term Holy Friday. That makes me think that the term, Good Friday, probably has to do with linguistic change, not the evolvement or application of a concept; hence, explanation #2 would be my choice with #1 also a possibility.

The Good Friday service is distinct from regular Mass. It has four parts and no recessional.

1. Stations of the Cross are an important part of Good Friday worship. The priest leads parishioners through those first. Not everyone comes to the Stations of the Cross on Good Friday, but most people do.

2. The Liturgy of the Word reenacts the passion of Jesus, beginning in the Garden of Gethsemane and ending with the crucifixion.

3. During the veneration of the cross everyone shows respect to the cross and gratitude and love for Jesus's sacrifice.

4. Communion is the regular Eucharist, in which all share the body and blood of Christ.

Photograph by Betty Lou Leaver

The Liturgy of the Word

The liturgy on Good Friday is long, but it is very important—and it is very interesting because parishioners take part in it. Everyone has a part in the story that never fails to evoke powerful emotions no matter how many times it is told.

The main part of the liturgy is the narration of the Passion of Jesus. A narrator from among the parishioners reads the story. The priest plays the part of Jesus. Selected parishioners (volunteers) play the parts of Peter and Pontius Pilate. Parishioners as a group play the part of the crowd.

The Passion narrative tells how Jesus spent time praying in the Garden of Gethsemane while the apostles slept. I get that; I think I might have fallen asleep, too. Jesus prayed all the way from Thursday night to Friday morning. He was disappointed that the apostles could not stay awake with him. I am afraid that he would be disappointed with me, too. Actually, I am sure there are things I do almost every day, though I try not to, that disappoint him—or things I do not do but should. Aren't we all lucky that he quickly forgives—and forgets!

The apostles did not know what was coming though Jesus had foretold much to them. They simply did not understand fully when he told them, and they did not have any sense of impending doom during the night in Gethsemane. Had they understood completely, they might not have slept at all!

Had they not slept, they would have realized the terrible strain Jesus was under. He sweat blood from the stress. He did not want to have to go through the passion, but he accepted God's will.

Sometimes I do not want to do what I know God wants me to do. I can be a naughty kitty! Usually, though, I do give in and do it. After all, the Boss never asks me to suffer the way He asked Jesus to suffer.

Terrible things happen after that all-night prayer in the garden. Judas brings the authorities to the garden to arrest Jesus. Jesus is brought up on trial. Pontius Pilate does not really want to condemn Jesus to death, but the crowd pushes him to do so.

Even Peter does not stand up for Jesus. Peter said he would never deny Jesus, but Jesus told him that he would, that before the cock crowed, he would deny him three times. Jesus was right. Peter did.

We have many roosters at the Mission. They are my friends, so I do not chase them. We live together in friendship, as equal creations of God. I get to listen to the Passion story by being at Mass and mingling with the parishioners. Sometimes, when no one in particular needs me, I sit with some of them, like my friends Jon and Juanita Mansmith, and I listen very carefully. I don't get to play a spectacular role, though, like my friends, the roosters. Almost always, when the narrator reads that a cock crowed, one of my rooster friends does crow—and he can be heard right on cue in the church.

Then, the story continues. The stations of the cross, done earlier, lay out each step of the journey. So does the Passion narrative as people read it during the Liturgy of the Word.

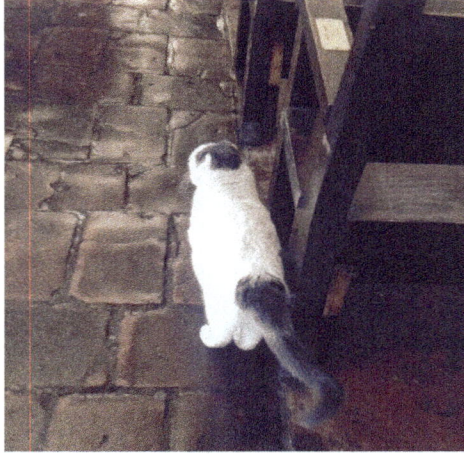

Photograph by Betty Lou Leaver

Veneration of the Cross

The veneration begins with the cross being brought down the aisle. When it reaches the altar, the cross is laid down, and the priest lies prostrate before the altar, in reverence and in recognition of the sorrow of the world at the crucifixion of Jesus. Parishioners then walk down the aisle. They take turns kissing the cross. In some churches, parishioners sing The Reproaches, which present Jesus's sorrow on the cross:

My people, what have I done to you?
or how have I grieved you?
Answer me!
Because I led you out of the land of Egypt,
you have prepared a cross for your Savior.

What more should I have done for you and have not done?
Indeed, I planted you as my most beautiful chosen vine
and you have turned very bitter for me,
for in my thirst you gave me vinegar to drink
and with a lance you pierced your Savior's side.

I exalted you with great power,
and you hung me on the scaffold of the cross.

During communion at Masses, I usually sit at the end of the pew to collect my pets as people walk past me on their way to the front of the church to take communion. I don't go down for obvious reasons: I cannot take communion (c'mon, I'm a cat). However, on Good Friday, I can go down with the parishioners and sit quietly, watching as each approaches the cross. It is a very solemn and sad part of the service.

Photograph by Anais Mora

Adoration of the Holy Cross

After the veneration of the cross, communion is distributed. And then the service ends very solemnly and very quietly with the stripping of the altar. After the final benediction, people walk out quietly, without talking. Only the cross remains.

If people want to stay and adore the cross after Mass, they can. Some do.

Because I live at the church, I am lucky. I can stay as long as I want on Good Friday and adore the cross. The silence that stays with me, like the silent part of every Mass, lets the Divine approach unimpeded by the external world.

Sometimes I stay a very long time. After all, this is the sad and wonderful story of my Boss's Son, who is one with my Boss, and therefore *is* my Boss. I love my Boss—and my Boss loves me—I could stay there forever, but I do have a mission that calls me back to the Mission Gift Shop until the next gathering of God's people for the Holy Saturday evening vigil.

EASTER VIGIL

Illustration by Uliana Yanovich

Sula, Parish Cat at Old Mission

What is Easter Vigil?

A vigil is a period of waiting. Easter Vigil is considered the greatest of all vigils and reflects the waiting that the disciples and especially the women who followed Jesus did after Joseph of Arimathea, having gotten permission from Pontius Pilate, laid Jesus in the tomb. They waited a very long time: three days. With Easter Vigil, the Triduum of Holy Thursday, Good Friday and Saturday Vigil is brought to a close. The waiting will end on Easter morning with the Resurrection.

That will be joyful. For now, though, we all wait. In sadness. In the dark.

Photograph by Stacey Gentry

Waiting before the Vigil

The church is always dark on Easter Vigil. I am among the first there, waiting not just for the Resurrection that is to come but also for the people who will be coming to wait together—they with me and I with them. I like greeting the people as they come in.

Often, I will know with whom I should be waiting. That, after all, is my mission.

Photograph by Betty Lou Leaver

The Mass

The Easter Vigil Mass is the third and last part of the three-day service that began on Holy Thursday. Like the Mass and service on the other days in the Triduum, Easter Vigil Mass is unique. It is not like any other Mass during the year.

The Vigil Mass is also complex—and rich. It goes from dark to light, from people who cannot see each other to people welcoming new members into the body of Christ. The Mass has four elements. These are

(1) the Service of Light;

(2) the Liturgy of the Word;

(3) Baptism; and

(4) the Liturgy of the Eucharist.

The Service of Light starts outside, around a fire. The parishioners surround the priest, who stands by the fire. The fire warms the parishioners and lights up the sky.

Then, the priest lights the Paschal candle. The Paschal candle reminds us that Jesus is the light of the world. From the Paschal candle several parishioners light their candles and then pass on the flame to each other until all candles are lit. The priest then proceeds into the church to the altar, followed by the parishioners with their lights.

I wait inside, in the dark, eagerly waiting for them to return with their lit candles showing them the way. The first part of the Mass is continued in the dark, with the only light coming from the candles.

The Liturgy of the Word recounts the history of salvation with seven readings from the *Old Testament* and two readings from the *New Testament* (one from the apostles and one from the Gospels). The homily usually focuses on the mysteries of salvation.

Baptism is always a very special part of the Easter Vigil Mass. At this time, both babies and people who have completed the Rite of Christian Initiation of Adults (RCIA) are baptized. For the adults, the Sacrament of Confirmation follows the Sacrament of Baptism.

The Mass concludes with the Eucharist. For the RCIA catechumens who have just been baptized and confirmed, the Eucharist becomes their first communion. A special night indeed, both for the new members of the parish and for all the parishioners welcoming new members.

A special night, too, for all it symbolizes in Catholic spirituality—salvation, *misterium*/mystery, and great love. A night as well for reconfirming our faith along with those confirming it for the first time. A time for feeling very close to my Boss. I certainly do!

Photograph by Lisa Lavagnino

Dismissal

The Vigil Mass ends late, but the waiting continues. It has been a long Mass, and everyone has gone home. I have completed my mission for the evening. Tomorrow a new day—a joyous day will dawn. For now, though, I sleep because I am tired. I understand how it was that the apostles fell asleep in the garden. I marvel that the women were able to keep vigil for so long.

EASTER

Illustration by Uliana Yanovich

Sula, Parish Cat at Old Mission

What is Easter?

Easter is a moveable feast and the greatest feast in the Catholic Church. Easter is the day when Mary Magdalene came to the tomb of Jesus and found it empty, at which time an angel told her that Yeshua (Jesus) had risen from the dead. (Yeshua, Jesus's given name in Hebrew, means *to rescue* or *to save*.) Through his death and resurrection, Jesus conquered evil and redeemed the world, as everyone says in reciting the stations of the cross, and showed himself to be the Christ (a title that means *messiah* in Hebrew and *anointed* or *chosen one* in Greek.) .

On Easter, churches are often decorated with Easter lilies (white lilies). Ours is. They symbolize the resurrection.

Historians estimate that the year of the crucifixion and resurrection was about 30 A.D. Yes, there is enough historical evidence that Jesus existed and approximately when.

Lent ends at the beginning of the Holy Thursday Mass, which begins the season of the Triduum. Easter is on the third day, a Sunday, after the end of Lent. The following week is considered Easter week. What a joyful time! Wouldn't it be nice if it could last all year? Well, at least, the season of Easter does last 50 days, all the way until Pentecost. (Pentecost is a great story, too; maybe I should write a book about Pentecost.)

Easter week ends with Divine Mercy Sunday. That comes from a vision seen by Saint Faustina Kowalska. (I described that in my book, *Saints I Know*, so if you want to know more about Saint Faustina, you could check that out—or just Google her.)

Both secular activities and religious activities are associated with Easter. Sometimes they get intertwined:

> People like to paint Easter eggs; various cultures have differing ways of making them.

> Cities often have Easter parades.

> The Easter bunny is a tradition that is shared broadly.

Some connections have been made between these traditions and Catholic beliefs, but they did, indeed, come from pagan celebrations of spring and new life—hence, the connection.

Photograph by Stacey Gentry

Easter Greetings

Easter dawns bright and early, and I am up to meet the sun. I wait impatiently for people to arrive at the church on Easter morning. The church is always packed, and the weather is almost always balmy. I can feel the mood of excitement and joy. I can also hear it in the words that people exchange: "Christ has risen" and, in response, "In truth, He has risen."

Photograph by James Caddell

Easter Mass

The Easter Mass tells the Easter story, the story of resurrection and hope and joy and triumph over death—all that is the very essence of our Catholic faith. The liturgy focuses on joy, and yes, the Alleluia is back!

When people receive the Eucharist—or so I hear them tell each other – they are thinking about new life, about putting off the old and putting on the new. The Eucharist comes into sharp focus on Easter Sunday as the body and blood of the *risen* Christ.

I love my mission on Easter Sundays. Happiness among the parishioners creates an almost electrified atmosphere. And, you know what? On most Easter Sundays, I am the one ministered to, not the other way around. It seems like all laps are open to me open to me, as if the spirit of giving has also been given new life on this glorious day. I feel especially blessed to be at my Mission on Easter Sunday, and I'm pretty sure that you would, too.

Sula, Parish Cat at Old Mission

MEMORIAL TO EVGENIY YANOVICH

Zhenya with his daughter, Julie
Photograph by his wife, Alla Yanovich

I want to dedicate this book to Evgeniy (Zhenya) Yanovich, the illustrator of my Christmas book. Even more, I want to share his exceptional story.

Sula, Parish Cat at Old Mission

Early Life

Evgeniy (Zhenya) was born in Akademgorodok, a tiny town like San Juan Bautista, outside the large city of Novosibirsk in Siberia. Akademgorodok, situated on the Ob River, is home to the Siberian Branch of the Russian Academy of Sciences, which is about all that is there, but that is enough. The Academy of Sciences is a special institute of some of the most talented scientists and researchers in Russia.

Zhenya was born with spina bifida. In 1979, Siberia had no access to antibiotics or the special treatments available to spina bifida children in some other parts of the world. Doctors held out no hope for Zhenya's survival, but he lived.

Early Talent

As he grew up, everyone in his town noticed Zhenya's artwork and the immense talent it showed. When his art came to the attention of professional artists, they recognized Zhenya's God-given gift, and the House of Scientists exhibited his work. He was only 12! He had other exhibits at the House of Scientists later. At the same time, he wrote poetry that was published in a book, and a documentary was made on his life in his midteen years.

The Beginning of Miracles

But, ultimately, he became very ill. His legs did not hold him up well enough to walk. Eventually, gangrene took over both of his legs and threatened his life. His parents began asking visitors to Novosibirsk to help.

About that time, my amanuensis, who had conducted research in Akademgorodok for her dissertation several years earlier, was conducting workshops for teachers in another Siberian city, Krasnoyarsk, and a delegation from Novosibirsk traveled there for the training. Zhenya's godmother, Natalia, headed the delegation.

As a result of their meeting, Zhenya arrived in California a year later. (It took a lot of paper work and a lot of time to get the US Embassy to agree to let him come.) While in the United States, Zhenya experienced a number of miracles, including unexpectedly meeting the head of the INS, who helped him get the right paperwork to stay in the USA (he had come with the wrong paperwork), touching the heart of the third richest man in the United States at the time (John Kluge), who paid for all his surgeries, and falling into the care of a nurse who used to be an art teacher, recognized his talent, and helped him to get a residency at the Virginia Center for Creative Arts, an honorary place for mature artists.

The miracle associated with the INS supervisor is that he met Zhenya at a prayer service before his first surgery, a double amputation of his diseased legs. The INS supervisor but had not planned to be at the holy day of obligation Mass. He usually attended a different church, but he got tied up at work and had to go to the closest one, which is where the priest prayed over Zhenya. Not only that, but this man had been an atheist 20 years earlier. He converted when his blind son received a miracle from a weeping icon and regained his sight.

The miracle of the billionaire, John Kluge, came in the form of redirected mail. The letter requesting Mr. Kluge's help was sent to Charlottesville, Virginia, but he lived in New York City. It took only three days for Mr. Kluge to receive the letter and send a check for half a million dollars to the hospital for Zhenya's care along with some money for new clothes and painting supplies—and then another $500,000 check a year later as Zhenya's expenses had mounted.

As for the artist nurse, Julie, how do you explain Zhenya falling into the care of someone with the very two specialties he needed? After some time, he even moved in with Julie, and he lived with her and her son for nearly 15 years before returning to Russia.

God very clearly loved Zhenya. Everyone could see that not only from the miracles I have already told you about but from even more that I do not have space to relate.

Going Home

Zhenya returned to Russia when his parents moved to Moscow. They were aging, and he wanted to be near them, to help them—and to be together with his six siblings. In Moscow, he married and fathered a daughter, whom he named after the nurse he had lived with in the United States.

Last summer, when his daughter was three years old, Zhenya took her and his wife to his dacha (summer house) in Burdenko near the Crimea in Ukraine. Like every Russian citizen, Zhenya got a month's annual vacaltion.

In Burdenko he began drawing the pictures for my Easter book, the book you have just finished reading. He took time off, however, to go to his sister's birthday party.

On the way to the party, he had a massive cerebral hemorrhage, totally unexpectedly. His relatives found a neurosurgeon to come to the local hospital. Given a very bad prognosis, the medical personnel transferred Zhenya to a very special hospital in Moscow, the one that Putin and all the Russian leaders use. The best doctors took care of Zhenya, but only a few days later, God welcomed him to his new home, Heaven.

I miss Zhenya very much. Everyone does. In only 42 years, he did so much and made so many, many friends, to whom he brought great joy!

I thought it important for you to know a little bit about his story. Because he touched my life, he has in a small way also touched your life. That is how God prompts us to build community among ourselves.

As for the pictures you see in this book, Uliana, Zhenya's youngest sister, stepped up when Zhenya's partially finished pictures could not be found and, in her own different and distinct style, drew illustrations of me for this book. I am so grateful!

If you liked this book and want to see lots more pictures, think about buying or borrowing my other books.

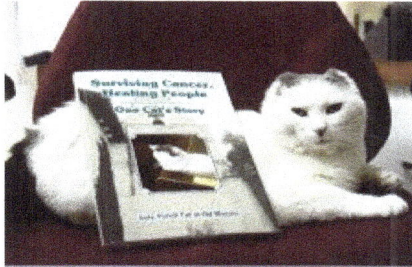

Surviving Cancer, Healing People: One Cat's Story. It is available at bookstores, on line, and at Old Mission San Juan Bautista and St. Francis Retreat Center in San Juan Bautista.

If your library does not have the book, please ask the acquisitions librarian to get a copy, not just for you but for any cat lovers and Mission lovers in your community and maybe, as well, those who want to spend some time reflecting on their faith.

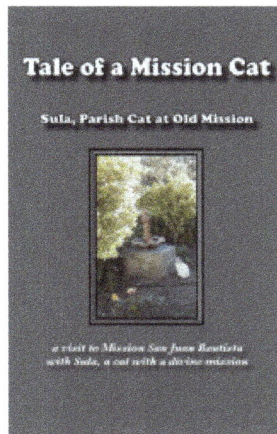

My second book, *Tale of a Mission Cat*, was written mainly for children. As it turned out, kids come in all ages, and many really big kids read this book. In the book, I introduce readers to Old Mission San Juan Bautista, my home—the church, the grounds, and the history.

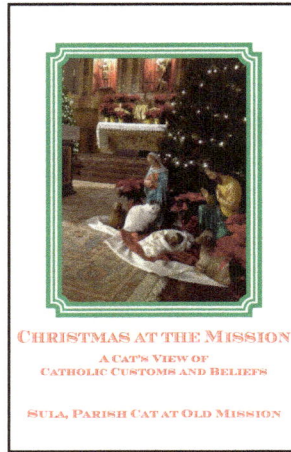

CHRISTMAS AT THE MISSION
A CAT'S VIEW OF
CATHOLIC CUSTOMS AND BELIEFS

SULA, PARISH CAT AT OLD MISSION

In December 2017, I wrote my first holiday book, called *Christmas at the Mission: A Cat's View of Catholic Customs and Beliefs.* I had a lot of fun writing it, learned a lot about Christmas and the source of Catholic customs, and delighted in the ways that Zhenya Yanovich, the Russian artist who illustrated the book, included me in each and every custom!

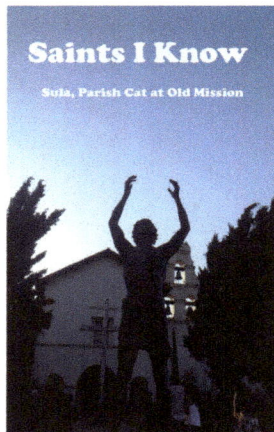

Saints I Know

Sula, Parish Cat at Old Mission

In June 2018, my latest book (before this one) came out. It was called *Saints I Know* and presents the saints that are the most important at Old Mission San Juan Bautista. You can read about their early lives and how they became saints. They were not always perfect, you know. And look at the last chapter—I make a prediction about future saints!

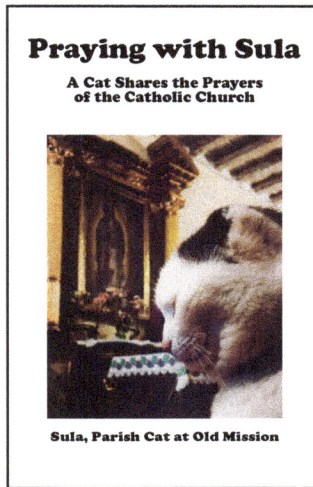

Praying with Sula

A Cat Shares the Prayers
of the Catholic Church

Sula, Parish Cat at Old Mission

I had such fun writing all these books that I don't want to stop. I am working on a book about prayer, all kinds of Catholic prayers. And I explain them. I want this book to be both informative and helpful. After all, prayer is how I talk to my Boss and how the parishioners talk to Him, too. That is one of the most important things in the world and in life.

As for me, you can read more stories about me and see more pictures here:

California Newspapers:

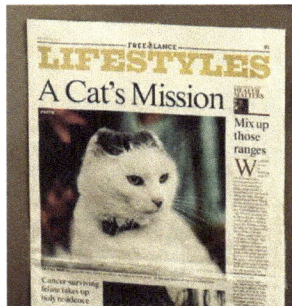

"A Cat's Mission." *Hollister Freelance* (Katie Helland, author; Nick Lovejoy/Studio Lovejoy, photographer). January 7 2016, pages B1, B15-16. http://www.sanbenitocountytoday.com/lifestyles/sula-the-cat-is-on-a-mission-in-san-juan/article_813c16f6-b575-11e5-886b-cfab711d8975. html

"Sula the Cat Is on a Mission in San Juan." Morgan Hill Times (Katie Helland). January 7, 2016. http://www.morganhilltimes.com/sula-the-cat/image_2a14d475-2f16-548a-a08d-62aa914fcd23.html (Yes, it is the same story—for different readers.)

Guideposts publications:

"Cat with a Mission." (Elizabeth Mahlou). *Guideposts Magazine*. December 2015. Pages 60-63 in *Guideposts*.

Photo by Martin Klimek Photography (Guideposts & ALL Creatures magazines)

"Family Room." *Guideposts Magazine*. December 2015, Pages 79-80.
"Sula, a Cat with a Divine Mission." https://www.guideposts.org/slideshow/sula-a-cat-with-a-divine-mission
"Cat with a Mission" was reprinted in All Creatures magazine as the feature story in the November-December 2017 issue.

Blog Interview:

My interview with Mudpie, the Cat: http://www.mochasmysteriesmeows.com/2016/09/mudpie-interviews-sula-old-mission-san.html
Most important, follow my adventures on my Face Book page, Sula, by friending me. Or, just like me! https://www.facebook.com/Sula-909598572467537/. More pictures! More stories! And I will answer you!

Old Mission San Juan Bautista

Founded June 24, 1797

P.O. Box 400, 406 Second Street, San Juan Bautista, CA 95045

Parish Website: www.oldmissionsjb.org

PARISH STAFF

Pastor: Alberto Cabrera
fralberto@oldmissionsjb.org

Manager: Magda Perino
Magda@oldmissionsjb.org

Secretary: Julie Borges
Bulletin Editor
julieb@oldmissionsjb.org

Religious Education: Mary Edge
faithformation@oldmissionsjb.org

RCIA: Sr. Dolores

Music Director: Edward J. DeGroot
denianded@sbcglobal.net

Gardener: Juan Ceja
Housekeeping: Kaleena Scargill
Maintenance: Joe Claus

Franciscan Sisters of the Atonement:
Sister Carmelita and Sister Dolores

Gift Shop/Visitor Center
giftshop@oldmissionsjb.org
Manager: Ana Silva

Gift Shop Retail Clerks:
Mary Anzar, Lorraine Castro,
Benito Garcia and Marie Reed

Mission Cat: Sula

Casa Maria Banquet Hall
William Medina
Phone.....831-593-5055
Fax.....831-593-5056
casamaria@oldmissionsjb.org

Bulletin Deadline Monday at 12 Noon Please include date, time, location along with contact name & phone number. **Fax to 831-623-2433** or send via email to julieb@oldmissionsjb.org

MASS SCHEDULE † HORARIO DE MISAS

SATURDAY VIGIL, ENGLISH ....5:00 P.M

SUNDAY, ENGLISH ....8:30 & 10:00 A.M.

DOMINGO, ESPAÑOL ....12:00 DE LA TARDE

WEDNESDAY-FRIDAY, ENGLISH ....8:00 A.M., CHAPI

CONFESSIONS ....SATURDAYS, 4:00 P.M., CHAP

Parish Office Hours
Monday thru Friday
9:00 am - 4:00 pm
(closed 12 Noon - 1:00 pm for lunch)

Mission Gift Shop & Visitor Center
Open 7 days a week
9:30 am - 4:30 pm

Contact Information
Parish Office.....831-623-2127
Parish Fax........831-623-2433
Religious Education...831-623-4178
Gift Shop/Visitor Center................831-623-45

Weddings or Baptisms
Contact the parish office or visit the parish we
(www.oldmissionsjb.org) for information.

Tips to keep our children safe:
Please do not allow your children to leave your sight while
Do not allow them to go to the restroom or out to the car
dren need to be supervised by a parent or adult at all tim
tending any church-related function.

Or come see me at Mass. I am always there! (As you can see if you look closely toward the bottom of the left-hand column on Old Mission Bulletin, I am officially the parish cat.)

What People Say about My Books

Surviving Cancer, Healing People: One Cat's Story

Surviving Cancer, Healing People: One Cat's Story is comprised of truly charming, heartwarming, endearing, and inspiring stories, shared by parishioners and told from the point of view of a lovable and amazingly insightful cat. [This] is one of those books that will linger in the mind and memory of the reader long after it is finished and set back upon the shelf. Heartwarming and thoughtful, *Surviving Cancer, Healing People* is a joy to browse and highly recommended. –

Reviewers' Choice/Small Press Bookwatch/
Midwest Book Review

Once you meet Sula through the pages of this book, you won't soon forget her. While it's Sula's "meowmoir," it's also the story of those whose lives she's impacted and an inside look at California's Spanish mission. Whether you're a religious person or not, the history is fascinating, and the connection she has with the people she's drawn to is undeniable. I've always said if there is such a thing as angels on earth, they come in the form of fur and four legs; at least, I know that's how they've always presented themselves in my own life. Sula is further proof of what I've suspected all along.

Melissa's Mochas, Mysteries,
and Meows blog

The inscription "Hic domus dei est et porta coeli," which means "This is the house of God and the gateway to heaven" towers over the portal to the church of Old Mission San Juan Bautista, greeting all who enter. But if guests happen to glance down, they might see a slightly rotund white cat with black markings and no ears. This would be Sula, the mission cat decreed by God, who he calls his Boss, to welcome all to the mission and to comfort those who are hurting. Sula knows about pain because he suffered through two bouts of cancer, having lost his ears in the process. *Surviving Cancer, Healing People: One Cat's Story* by Sula Parish Cat at Old Mission was written and photographed by staff and friends of the mission, but cleverly presented in the voice of Sula. As we learn about Sula, we also learn about the mission as well as St. Francis' Friars Minor and the Sisters of Atonement. As a tourist destination, the mission calls to all to come to the table and worship. To quote Fr. Jerry from Sula, "the Table is ready, and all are invited." *Surviving Cancer, Healing People: One Cat's Story* was written to raise funds for the Old Mission San Juan Bautista. Because the over-200-year-old mission sits on top of the intersection of three fault lines, earthquakes have struck twice in the past and each tremor has weakened it. Beyond being a fundraiser, though, the book is an inspirational call to worship. This little book about Sula, the mission cat, not only weaves short sermons into each chapter, but gives a short history of the mission of San Juan Bautista. We learn why cat doors were installed, why the church doors were built so high, and why the church was arranged around the sun of the winter solstice. Thanks to the great writing, photography and editing, the book flows nicely and leaves the reader with a positive and peaceful feeling. Loved this little book! I want to go to the mission now and visit with Mr. Sula in person. I highly recommend this sweet little book to all readers.

Claudia Coffey (Readers' Favorite)

I LOVED this book and highly recommend it. Sula the cat lives at Old Mission in California, a Franciscan mission which needs many repairs from past earthquakes and to secure it for another one. The book is part of a fundraiser for those efforts. Sula takes her job very seriously at the mission. She visits a statue of St. Francis every day where she learns of what her duties are that day and who needs her the most. She then enters the church and sits with those people during mass. As a Catholic (somewhat lapsed) I enjoyed reading about the mass, but you don't have to be any particular religion to read this. Sula is mainly white and the California sun has not been good to her. She has had to have surgery for cancer on her ears twice so she doesn't have ears anymore, but that doesn't stop her from loving everyone and everyone loving her.

15 and Meowing blog

There have always been cats living at the Old Mission San Juan Bautista. It is one of twenty-one Spanish missions in southern California built by the Franciscan order. Round holes were cut into its heavy doors during construction. Early cats were welcomed to hunt mice, but the current parish cat, Sula, has been tasked with a different mission. Every day this big, white Turkish Van cat reports to the garden statue of St. Francis of Assisi, a lover of all animals... and people. In this book, Sula claims to receive orders concerning which church visitors need the comfort of a cat companion on any given day. Regardless of how she recognizes her charges, Sula instinctively approaches someone in need. It might be a communicant taking confession for the last time before joining her departed spouse. It may be visitors who arrive at the mission in time for a mass. She sits quietly at their feet or climbs onto a lap. Perhaps it is someone who has read Sula's story online and has come to meet and pet this now famous cat. Why is she famous? Sula is a cancer survivor. She has lost both ears due to melanoma skin cancer and resulting surgeries. (Two parishioners took care of her during that time.) Like any human might, Sula enjoys spending a great deal of time outside in the bright California sun. Being a survivor, she now attracts people who have or did have cancer themselves. The mission's gift shop office is Sula's official place of residence. The team there has encouraged the telling of her story, and that of some parishioners, in books and magazine articles.

Donna Ford (US Review of Books; Recommended)

I loved this book. Sula the cat lives at a mission in California. She visits a statue of St. Francis daily where she learns who she should spend time with that day. She goes in the church during mass time and visits with those she senses could use some love. She also visits with people in the gift shop and on field trips. Poor Sula has lost her ears from skin cancer, but that doesn't make her any less lovable. The mission has been through earthquakes and is in need of repairs if it is to stay standing through another one. Sula wrote this book to help raise funds for this. If you love cats, you will definitely love this book.

Ellen Pitch (Goodreads)

A Wise and Eminently Sane Cat, May 5, 2017. Sula is a feline inhabitant of the Old Mission San Juan Bautista in California. Her personal mission is to bring comfort and reassurance to those who need to experience God's love in a tangible way. She selects individuals in the church and sits by them or on their laps during services. She accompanies visitors as they tour the grounds or walk the stations of the cross. This charming book is full of lovely photos of Sula fulfilling her mission as well as her reflections as she does so. Sula is wise and eminently sane. She has learned to grieve (for the loss of her ears due to cancer) without becoming stuck in grief. She has learned the joy of helping others and lovingly seeks to offer comfort and aid whenever she can. At the same time, she has learned to gratefully accept help when she is in need. She has learned to look for silver linings in the darkest clouds. When she had to wear a cone after her cancerous ears were removed, she was forced to find unusual ways of eating from her bowl. Sula said this helped her to understand that physically and mentally handicapped parishioners face additional challenges and also need to find alternative ways of doing things. The experience increased her acceptance and understanding of others. Her faith is strong and she trusts her maker. The Old Mission surrounds her with reminders of His love and care. She is grateful and content. Her example serves as a reminder to seek the things that can make us truly joyful. I would love to have a friend like Sula.

Charles Lord (Amazon review)

Sweet Cat on a mission to save a Mission, August 22, 2016. I loved this book. This is a memoir of sorts written by Sula, a cat that lives at a mission in California. She takes her work of communing with people very seriously. All day, every day she spends visiting with people in the church, gift shop and walking around the mission grounds. The California sun has been harsh on her. Poor Sula has had surgery twice to remove cancer on her ears. Despite no longer having ears, she is still adorable and loving. The mission has been around a long time, through many earthquakes which has weakened the structure. Sula has written this book to raise funds to help do the work necessary to keep it from falling down. This book is a must read for all cat lovers. I know all Catholics would enjoy it as well, but that is not a requirement to read it :)

Amazon customer (Amazon review)

Tale of a Mission Cat

Remarkable Sula! Love that Supercat!
Kris Maas (Sula fan)

All reader reviews have been 5 stars! Thank you, readers!

Letter to the Reader

Dear Reader,

Would you take a little time to help me get the word out about me, my books, and Old Mission San Juan Bautista? While the Mission certainly needs money, not everyone is in a position to contribute financially. I understand that. I am only a cat. I can only contribute through my book sales and people donating in my name.

Nearly anyone can contribute in a big way that does not cost anything. Write a review of one of my books—or of all of them! Reviews are the best way to share your opinion of the books and to get the word out to others. Post it on Amazon, Barnes & Noble, Twitter, Face Book, a blog somewhere, or your own website and send me the link. That would help me ever so much!

And if you would like to communicate with me directly, there are two ways: my Facebook page (just type in Sula pet, and it will pop up) or through MSI Press, where the editor monitors my fan mail: editor@msipress.com.

Thank you for helping out! Thank you for being my friend!
Your friend,
Sula

Proceeds from this book will be used to help restore, retrofit, and preserve Old Mission San Juan Bautista.

Tax-deductible contributions may be made online to the fund at www.oldmissionsjb.org. Or, a check made out to "Save Mission San Juan Bautista" may be mailed to

Old Mission San Juan Bautista
P. O. Box 400
San Juan Bautista, CA 95045

Please note, if you don't mind, that this is a donation in the name of Sula—unless, of course, you prefer to donate in the name of someone special to you. All donations are welcome!

Thank you for helping to save my home!
Sula